Brain Research and the Split Brain Theory

Brain research, once an esoteric subject, has recently become a concern of many groups, including educators who have been particularly intrigued with findings about the split brain theory. This theory holds that the right hemisphere carries out intuitive, holistic, and simultaneous operations (such as creative imagining), and the left carries out linear, sequential, and verbal operations (such as reading and calculating). Most schooling tends to emphasize the left hemisphere and neglect the right. Consequently, educators are currently examining the split brain or hemispheric theory to determine its impact on instructional practices. This fastback summarizes current brain research, especially as it applies to the split brain theory, and probes some of the implications of this theory for balanced curricula and instruction. Also, we have included a report on the development and application of the theory of human consciousness as substantiated by split brain research and the effects of cultural and educational influences.

The Brain

The brain is perhaps the least understood part of the anatomy. It has puzzled man for thousands of years. Researchers are fascinated by its mystery and complexity.

The average brain weighs only about three pounds and contains billions of neuron and neuroglia cells arranged in layers. A single neuron cell contains millions of RNA molecules. Each molecule of RNA is capable of converting genetic instructions from DNA (also present in the cell) into any of 100,000 proteins. The brain has an electrical system that can be traced on an electroencephalograph. The signal, measured in millionths of a volt, is picked up by wires attached to the scalp. The brain also has a chemical system composed of neurotransmitter chemicals that either transmit or block the electrical impulses. Thus the brain is a system many times more complex than the most sophisticated computer. It is simultaneously conscious of its existence and adaptable to it. In this small, soft, grayish lump of tissue are generated dreams, feelings, and learning.

Research studies have determined that the human brain is in fact two organs rather than one (Gazzaniga, 1975).* These two parts or hemispheres, while seemingly alike, have unique characteristics. On the basic levels of body function the hemispheres work alike in that each carries half of the load. The right hemisphere controls the motor and sensory operations of the left side of the body, the left hand, and half of each retina. (Images in the left visual field are projected to the right hemisphere.) The left hemisphere controls the same operations on the right side of the body. Although the hemispheres operate independently, they are connected by a bundle of nerve tissue called the corpus callosum. The corpus callosum integrates the operations of the two hemispheres, in effect letting the right hand know what the left hand is doing.

In addition to lateral motor and perceptual control, each hemisphere has been found to specialize in a different mode of consciousness. In normal humans this is not apparent, because the corpus callosum acts as an integrator. Reality is not clearly cut into two separate realms of consciousness. But experiments on brain-injured patients and people who have had the corpus callosum severed for medical reasons indicate that two separate and unique ways of processing stimuli exist within one person, and each seems to stem from a separate hemisphere. Laboratory tests of normal, uninjured people using a surface electroencephalograph have found that normal people also utilize the specializations of the two hemispheres.

---

*Full citations for references in the text may be found in the Selected References at the end of this fastback.

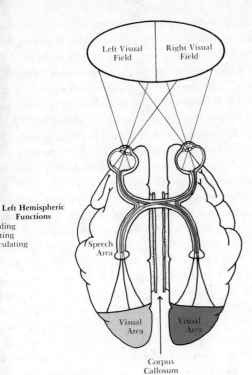

Left Hemispheric Functions
Reading
Writing
Calculating

Speech Area

Visual Area

Right Hemispheric Functions
Art
Media
Meditation

Visual Area

Corpus Callosum

Modal Descriptors
Linear
Sequential
Verbal
Analytic
Rational
Propositional
Explicit
Logical

Modal Descriptors
Simultaneous
Holistic
Visual-spatial
Synthetic
Metaphoric
Appositional
Tacit
Intuitive

An Outline of the Brain

The difference between the hemispheres seems to lie in the manner in which each receives stimuli and processes it. R. W. Sperry theorizes that the left hemispheric mode specializes in linear, sequential, and analytic operations. The right hemispheric mode includes simultaneous, holistic, spatial, and intuitive operations. Language, a linear function, is directed by the left hemisphere for almost all right-handed people and half of the left-handed population. Reading, writing, and computation are acknowledged as left hemispheric functions. Nonverbal and metaphoric thought originate in the right hemisphere, as does the ability to perceive many stimuli simultaneously and form impressions. (See diagram on page 9.)

Thus the two dominant modes of consciousness are the right hemispheric (simultaneous) and the left hemispheric (linear) processing systems. Functions of the modes are activities associated with one of the two. For example, reading, writing, and arithmetic are among the functions of the left hemispheric mode that utilize the linear/sequential processing system. Art, visual media, and metaphor are functions of the holistic right hemispheric mode of consciousness. There seems to be a hemispheric preference for specific functions in most individuals. However, at times a function can be lateralized in the opposite hemisphere or even show mixed dominance. For example, most language has simultaneous parts, as is seen in much poetry, and there are many sequential elements in spatial perception. Although the language function may lateralize primarily in the left hemisphere, it is not exclusively left hemispheric, as demonstrated by people in other cultures and people who have had the left hemisphere of their brains damaged. In these cases the right hemisphere has taken over the language function. Once information enters the brain, both hemispheres can work cooperatively to process it. Specialization in the hemispheres does occur, however, in the modes of consciousness, if not always for particular functions.

Human Consciousness

The modes of human consciousness need further exploration in light of developments in hemispheric brain theory. The use of the left hemisphere for linear and sequential functions has been prevalent throughout human history. The use of the right hemisphere for simultaneous and intuitive processes has also existed throughout the development of mankind. Until recent times, people have had to struggle for survival and for basic needs. The search for clothing, shelter, safety, and food occupied most of one's energy. Left hemispheric functions of analysis and sequence were the skills that permitted early man to survive and develop. These early developments initiated the theory of the supremacy of analytical and sequential thought as the prevalent mental process. Thinking in an analytical and sequential manner continues to be the most respected process used by the intellectual community in dealing with the world.

Although rational analysis has helped people survive and grow, it has also presented problems for contemporary civilization. Problems with population, pollution, energy, ecology, and medicine are the result of linear thought processes. Solutions to these problems are continually advocated but are usually linear, piecemeal answers. Only parts of problems are solved, not complete ones, and often more problems are created by the solutions. For example, man-made energy users, created to make life easier and more comfortable, have begun to exhaust our natural resources. Synthetic foods, created for convenience in use and storage, may have harmful side effects. Technological methods of food production have eliminated starvation as a major problem for most of the world but have made obesity a common problem in many Western countries. The automobile has given people great geographic mobility but has created pollution and energy problems.

Thus linear solutions to complex questions have provided only partial answers. The rational/linear process is not always the appropriate problem-solving mode. What is needed, suggests Robert Ornstein in *The Mind Field*, is a shift from the linear processes, which are egocentric and focus on individual analysis, to the processes that focus holistically and simultaneously on general relationships and can provide solutions to complex, collective problems. Ornstein states that "consciousness could convey a more comprehensive perspective of the life and action of an individual and of a group, as well as the relationships among seemingly disparate activities and systems." The development of the right hemispheric mode of consciousness, which exhibits wholeness, simultaneity, and intuition, will not be easy. The left hemisphere's rational, linear, sequential mode is ingrained in people's intellectual functioning and to this point has served well in advancing a technological civilization. It is now necessary, however, to utilize the right hemisphere processes in attempting to solve complex problems in contemporary society.

It is hoped that new explorations into human consciousness and educational approaches will provide support for those people who, maybe without knowing it, have developed and urged others to develop both modes of consciousness. These people have always been small in number and their contributions have not always been widely noted. The mainstream in Western culture in recent times has turned further away from holistic approaches and has left a void in the completeness of human consciousness and in their schooling modes. In this fastback we should like to develop and encourage an integrated and balanced perspective toward consciousness and schooling.

A Balanced Curriculum

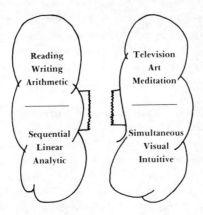

Reading
Writing
Arithmetic

Television
Art
Meditation

Sequential
Linear
Analytic

Simultaneous
Visual
Intuitive

In most schools the linear and sequential processes of the left hemisphere of the brain virtually dominate the curriculum and instructional methodology. Linear thinking is also prevalent in nonschool situations. Schools have been a primary conveyor of the linear/sequential mode of consciousness and its functions. In order to develop both the linear and holistic modes of consciousness, schools need to evaluate their curricula and instructional practices. This section suggests ways to evaluate curriculum in order to balance the functions performed by the left and right hemispheres.

A school curriculum that is weighted toward subjects that utilize the linear/sequential mode of the left hemisphere of the brain is imbalanced. This imbalance is brought about by the emphasis on left hemisphere functions such as reading, writing, and arithmetic, while right hemispheric functions such as art, music, and drama are often ignored. Moreover, the "back-to-basics" movement is likely to assure that the left hemisphere will continue to be emphasized over the right.

Various balances should be considered in the construction of a curriculum. Traditionally, balances have included such factors as the nature of individual learners and how they learn, cognitive and affective components of teaching/learning experiences, social and psychological aspects of growth and development, and balance between social demands and individual needs. Split brain research and current curricular trends suggest also that the curriculum should be examined in relation to left/right hemisphere specialization and integration. A balanced curriculum is one that educates the modes of consciousness of both hemispheres through use of the multiple processing systems of the brain.

Right Hemisphere Implications for Curriculum

What does the traditional curriculum require of students? They may begin the day by following verbal directions to accomplish a linear task. They may be asked to read certain material and then write the answers in response to written questions. They may compute a page of math problems. The teacher is generally pleased if students do all of these tasks correctly, and may describe them as superior students, working to the best of their abilities. But in reality these students are using only half of their potential, half of their thinking ability, half of their brains. The brain's right hemisphere receives little, if any, organized, deliberate schooling (Bogen, 1975). Our Western, rationally oriented culture tends to revolve around and depend upon linear and sequential activities. Educators need to develop systematic and sophisticated curricula that facilitate the multiple processing systems of the brain. Perhaps some who appear to be slow learners are slow only in regard to left hemisphere functions; they may be very capable right hemisphere learners.

(Photograph by Emily Luecke)

The linear functions of the brain are developed by subjects such as reading, writing, and arithmetic.

In school almost all subject matter is taught through reading. In most classes the first act of the teacher is to distribute the textbook. But there are other legitimate (perhaps even superior) methods of teaching and learning than reading, and there are other legitimate means of demonstrating competence than linearly dominant paper-and-pencil tests. In spite of this fact, most schools seem to advocate reading almost exclusively as the method of teaching and testing. Although this methodology works for students who are verbally facile, it may work a tremendous hardship on those who are intelligent but not language oriented.

The failure of many remedial reading programs may be attributed to this one-sided (left hemisphere) effort. What is often needed for students exhibiting reading problems is a balanced (linear/simultaneous) approach. This argument is not a denunciation of reading and reading teachers, but rather an effort to stimulate interest in a hemispherically balanced approach to reading and curriculum that legitimizes right hemispheric modes of learning as genuine, scientific, and necessary.

Balancing the Curriculum

The balanced curriculum suggested by split brain research can be implemented, at least in part, through interdisciplinary approaches. Adding subjects that require right hemisphere dominance to the curriculum can provide the increased stimulation needed for the right hemisphere and also the content integration needed for a balanced curriculum. Perhaps traditional obstacles to interdisciplinary approaches will be overcome as split brain research provides a catalyst for the development of interdisciplinary studies. The value of interdisciplinary approaches has been recognized by educators for years, but specialization, despite its drawbacks, has ruled.

Another method of balancing the curriculum may come from the introduction of learning experiences outside the traditional school curriculum. Experiences that are currently popular outside of formal schooling include meditation in its many forms: TM, yoga, Sufi, biofeedback, biorhythms, and hypnosis. People are flocking to these classes for the personal fulfillment claimed for a "wonder weekend" of meditation. These popular, holistic, and metaphoric experiences and

16

(Photograph by Emily Luecke)

The holistic and simultaneous functions of the right hemisphere must be developed through school curricula and instructional methodologies.

17

others like them suggest that many people are right hemisphere illiterates in need of training and are seeking this training outside of school. Perhaps schools should recognize that such a deficit exists in their curricula and make the needed changes.

An additional reason for hemispheric balance in the curriculum is the impact of television and other electronic media on students before and after they enter school. Many children have sat before the electronic baby sitter for hundreds of hours before entering school, and television has become an integral part of their lives. In most classrooms, however, not only is television ignored, but all right hemispheric visual stimuli are often absent.

The College Entrance Examination Board's advisory panel, chaired by Willard Wirtz, recently reported on the decline of the Scholastic Aptitude Test scores. One factor mentioned by the panel as contributing to the decline in test scores was television. The panel acknowledged that it could not prove that television contributes to the decline, but confidently asserted the conviction that it does. Noting the vast number of hours the average person spends watching television, the panel suggested that television has become "surrogate parent, substitute teacher," and that the considerable amount of time formerly devoted to homework, reading, and writing is now spent watching television.

Despite the panel's insistence that television is one of the factors responsible for the decline of the SAT scores, the committee also noted that "a good deal more of most children's learning now develops through viewing and listening than through traditional modes." Members of the panel expressed the conviction that television and related forms of communication "give the future of learning its largest promise."

Although the above data can be interpreted in various ways (including an attack on the unchanging and linear SAT), the panel's report emphasizes the dichotomy between the design of school curricula and tests, which are linearly dominant, and television, which is visual and simultaneous. A possible solution to this conflict and the resultant test score decline that is congruent with split brain research is not a one-sided, back-to-the-basics movement but school curricula that utilize learning modes of both hemispheres of the brain. This utilization and integration of the hemispheric modes will increase visual and simultaneous skills and augment linear and sequential processes in school curricula.

In addition to the cultural prejudice against having curriculum activities that stimulate the right hemisphere of the brain, there has been an educational prejudice against right hemisphere activities that tend to free students to think for themselves. Student control is secured through linear methods, not through metaphoric methods that stress creativity and nonconformity. However, the biographies of many geniuses show them to be persons who develop both modes of consciousness and who create an electric synergy between the modes. Robert Ornstein, in the *Psychology of Consciousness*, summarizes this education transition by stating that

> the shift from the individual, analytic consciousness to a holistic mode,
> brought about by training the intuitive side of ourselves . . . consists of a
> breaking down of the contracts which maintain personal consciousness,
> and a transition from this analytic mode to the emergent, "gestalt" mode
> of consciousness.

Developing both the linear and holistic modes of consciousness in students through balanced curricula will increase student achievement.

Student Evaluation

To determine the effectiveness of a hemispherically balanced curriculum, a change in the process of student evaluation must take place. Evaluation, both teacher-developed and standardized, is generally based on the student's ability to deal with linear and sequential functions. Moreover, on most tests facility with language is paramount. Tests that use visual language instead of verbal language are rare. As part of student evaluation, nonlanguage-based tests need to be constructed in order to give those who are right hemisphere dominant a greater opportunity to demonstrate their intelligence. It is likely that many students are being misjudged because of an inability to deal with the left hemisphere functions in most tests currently used for measuring content. Tests should be developed to measure those children who are oriented visually and metaphorically but not verbally. Many students may increase their scores when such tests are used.

After students are tested, results are usually recorded on linear report cards. Percentages, letters, and numbers constitute a linear scale of achievement. The numbers are then translated into sequential orders, otherwise known as honor rolls, dean's lists, etc., that encourage competition and comparison. Seldom are right hemisphere operations used to evaluate or to report evaluations of students. Perhaps evaluation is an area where the simultaneous and holistic mode can be developed and utilized in schools to overcome some of the inadequacies of current grading practices.

Examination of Curriculum

In order to develop curricula that provide left hemisphere/right hemisphere balance, the following questions (based on the previously stated rationale) will prove helpful.

1. Do subjects in the curriculum utilize equally the modes of both hemispheres of the brain?

2. Are major questions asked that extend beyond linear thought and require the use of the multiple processing systems of the brain?

3. In line with the two-hemisphere theory, does the curriculum provide for an integrated approach to learning?

4. Does the testing program provide for the child whose dominant literacy is visual?

These questions constitute guidelines for evaluating curricula to determine left/right hemisphere balance. A swing of the educational pendulum to the right hemisphere to compensate for the previous emphasis on the left hemisphere could be destructive. Interrelatedness between the hemispheres is the key to balanced curricula and a fully functioning brain.

The Western scientific mode of linear and sequential processes develops only one-half of the brain and limits the kinds of questions that can be asked. A balanced curriculum that integrates right hemisphere and left hemisphere modes will not only foster full brain development but will stimulate new kinds of questions and provide a fuller understanding of the human experience based on complementary modes of consciousness.

Balanced Instructional Strategies

Individual teachers may be powerless to change the curriculum in their schools. At best these teachers may be free to teach any number of topics within a prescribed subject. At worst they may be given a predetermined list of facts to be learned in a prescribed sequence. In either case they have a certain freedom to use their own instructional methods to present material. If a teacher is concerned with integrated learning, then the curricular restrictions can be overcome by using methods of instruction that stimulate and develop both hemispheres of the brain.

Educators have long been aware that students learn in different ways. The current knowledge about the two hemispheres of the brain suggests that one difference among learners involves preference for processing input with one hemisphere or the other. This preference is somewhat analogous to left- and right-handedness. A left-handed person uses that hand to write or draw, and a left brain dominant person prefers verbal instructions to visual instructions. However, as most tasks are done more skillfully and efficiently when both hands work together, so thinking is augmented by both hemispheres working together.

Teachers need to determine the preferred mode of learning for each student and when presenting material should direct the explanation toward the preferred mode. This technique is not new to most educators and has long been recommended in special education. The teacher must provide visual as well as verbal stimulation to students. In effect, the teacher must try to reach as many senses as possible, so that each

(Photograph by Emily Luecke)

Classroom drama integrates both modes of consciousness. In this classroom students are learning grammar through drama.

learner has an opportunity to perceive new knowledge through the preferred mode.

In addition, the teacher should provide experiences that encourage the secondary hemisphere to acquire skills. Thus both modes develop and the learner uses his whole brain in a manner similar to the way a pianist uses both hands, one playing the main theme while the other plays the accompaniment, creating a whole product.

To teach with the deliberate intent of utilizing both hemispheres of the brain, the instructor must assume the following responsibilities:

1. Each student must be assessed to determine the preferred mode of thinking. A teacher can usually observe which student is an avid reader and writer but dislikes gym class, or which one can take a bicycle apart in five minutes but shows no interest in mathematics. Another aspect of this assessment is the amount of success the student is currently experiencing in school. In the linearly oriented educational system where reading, writing, and math are most valued, students who learn in a linear way tend to be better students, while those whose learning dominance is in the visual/spatial mode may be labeled slow learners or low achievers. Members of the second group have little chance to learn in the easiest way for them.

2. The teacher is obligated to introduce new material in both a linear and a visual/spatial manner. This permits the individual to grasp the new material more easily, because he is more secure in learning in his preferred manner. This method of instruction does not necessarily require two separate lesson plans and two different sets of materials. It requires that a teacher give visual/spatial instruction as well as verbal. It may mean pantomiming directions while giving them verbally. Role playing can be helpful in some situations. Overhead transparencies, charts, maps, and manipulable objects can help visualize verbal concepts. One need not separate these materials into those for the linearly oriented and those for the visually oriented. Given a choice, most students use the more comfortable mode, but it is helpful for them to think also in their nonpreferred mode.

3. To stimulate both modes, occasionally the teacher should consciously present material in only one. An example would be to aim solely at the left hemisphere by reading a passage with no visual stimu-

lation. Or a holistic hemispheric stimulus may involve using a slide-tape show with music to explain a concept. Individual students may also be assigned specific work to give them practice in stimulating their nonpreferred mode.

Another resource that may be overlooked—even refuted as an educational tool—is television. It is invaluable for teachers who are concerned with the development of both hemispheres, for of all instructional media it is foremost in providing simultaneous stimulation. The programming, of course, must fully use the verbal and visual/spatial potential of television.

Recent educational television programming has become much more creative than it was when the instructor read a lecture while standing before the camera. National programs such as "Sesame Street" and "Electric Company" are but two examples of effective use of the medium. Local public broadcasting stations often have extensive educational programming for a wide range of age levels and subject areas. Many school districts have videotape equipment to record shows that are televised at times other than during school hours.

Because of the pervasiveness of television in our culture, students can readily relate to it. Educators would do well to recognize this. Instead of deriding television as a medium, educators should take action against empty programming and support productions which effectively utilize the potential of television and encourage total brain stimulation.

Balanced Programs

According to a 25-member panel reporting in a two-year survey, *Coming to Our Senses: The Significance of the Arts for American Education*, students in school programs offering a curriculum balanced between right and left hemisphere activities have produced higher test scores in the basic areas. Intermediate students in the "Learn To Read Through the Arts" program in New York (funded by the Guggenheim Museum and Title I) showed significant gains in reading scores measured by standardized tests. Fourth-, fifth-, and sixth-grade students took part in the program, which relates art and reading activities through use of the Guggenheim Museum's collection. Students at the

(Photograph by Emily Luecke)

Technology provides assistance in utilizing the individual learning styles of students.

Mosswood Mini-School in Oakland, California, who attend art classes six to eight times more often than students in most schools made math and reading gains at significantly higher rates than other students. The "Interdisciplinary Model Program in the Arts for Children and Teachers" (IMPACT) in Columbus, Ohio, reports that participating students gained in reading and math ability and showed superior problem-solving ability.

These results support Rudolf Arnheim's suggestion that man's visual thinking makes his verbal thinking possible. Arnheim believes that some ideas can best be expressed visually (e.g., without using your hands, try to describe water going down a drain) and that in many instances visual expression is superior to verbal.

The split brain theory supports the inclusion of holistic subjects in the curriculum as well as instructional methods that employ holistic and visual/spatial strategies. Brain research, lower verbal test scores, and results of the combined arts and basic skills programs all indicate that visual literacy is rapidly becoming as important as verbal literacy in our society and must be recognized in schools. A need exists for the exploration of how visual skills can improve instruction and how they can best support and encourage learning in all areas of instruction.

Here are some guidelines for teachers to follow if they are interested in developing both visual and verbal thought:

1. Encourage the student to picture concepts or objects visually before giving verbal answers.

2. When giving assignments, give students the choice of illustrating the idea or writing it in words.

3. Try to give explanations both visually and verbally.

4. Courses in art, music, and physical education should not be considered diversionary, routine-breaking activities. Incorporate them into the more linear subjects and vice versa.

5. Aim, occasionally, to stimulate only one hemisphere of the brain.

6. Be aware of each student's preferred tendency to think linearly or holistically.

Math

Math, a linear subject, also involves visual thinking in the computational process and in higher logic. Simple computation is often presented to students in graphic situations, but generally the use of words is involved. For example, subtraction may be presented to a second-grade student with a problem like this: "There were two bones. A dog took one. How many were left?" The same problem could be presented in this manner:

The student may answer with the numeral "one," may draw a bone, or may make a mental leap to another conclusion (such as "The dog got sick."). Such problems interspersed with more traditional ones encourage both right hemispheric and left hemispheric operations.

In the area of geometry, manipulables and drawings are traditional because geometry is a more visual/spatial discipline. However, students are often asked to respond linearly. They should be encouraged to draw and construct answers to geometric problems, perhaps even drawing proofs in addition to listing theorems.

Visual logic as well as verbal logic can be developed. Pattern detection, finding hidden figures, categorizing, and ordering all involve logic and can be encouraged through visual exercises such as mazes, picture analogies, pencil puzzles, and cube games. Mental, visual problems encourage logical use of imagery. Here is an example:

"Shut your eyes. Think of a wooden cube such as a child's block. It is painted. Now imagine that you take two parallel and vertical cuts through the cube, dividing it into equal thirds. Now take two additional vertical cuts, at 90° to the first ones, dividing the cube into equal ninths. Finally, take two parallel and horizontal cuts through the cube, dividing it into twenty-seven cubes. Now, how many of these small cubes are painted on three sides? On two sides? On one side? How many cubes are unpainted?" (This problem comes from a very useful book, *Experiences in Visual Thinking*, by Robert H. McKim.)

Science

Science can be readily applied to both hemispheres of the brain through an investigative activity approach to learning concepts. By first performing the experiments and then tabulating and observing the results, students can learn in a balanced way. The teacher can make a conscious effort to present concepts nonverbally and then question the students and receive verbal responses from them.

For example, a teacher might light two candles and put a jar over one—all without speaking. Students can then question the teacher and suggest reasons why they think the candle inside the jar went out while the other continued to burn. After this they can try the experiment themselves to see whether their hypotheses are correct. For example, if someone thinks the flame went out because the bottom of the jar touched the flame, repeating the experiment with a larger jar would rule out this hypothesis. They can draw diagrams to illustrate their own investigations. Students can gain in linear skills by verbalizing and writing down their observations and results.

Providing problems without answers requires alternative modes of thinking and encourages reliance on intuition. The ability to make these mental leaps is a characteristic of most great scientists and is responsible for many discoveries. Asking students why the plant by the window grows better than the plant in the corner requires that they use observational skills to determine the difference between the two plants and make some intuitive guesses about the answer.

Language Arts

Language exists in both verbal and visual forms. Visual language follows a grammar and syntax as real as verbal language. It is often more real to television-oriented students. Picture sentences and stories can often be used to teach verbal concepts. Students just learning to read and write can use combinations of pictures and words to communicate their ideas, as can those who have difficulty with written communication.

Grammar can be effectively taught through the use of pantomime. Students realize without being told that verbs are action words, because when they pantomime such words they are moving physically. Prepositions can be understood as direction words because students find themselves giving directions when required to pantomime these words.

Poetry can help learners make their verbal images more visual. By having students draw or photograph their ideas of such abstract words as *happy, sad, troublesome,* or *lonely,* the teacher encourages creative visual imagery, which is the essence of all poetry. Literary terms such as "mood," "theme," "crisis," and "conflict" can be actively approached by student-created media. A single-concept super-8mm film is inexpensive to produce and involves many of the same organizational skills as writing a single concept theme.

Social Studies

In social studies a balanced and visual approach gives students a complete feeling of other cultures. Comparing cultures and finding differences and reasons for differences require developed visual skills. Pictures, films, and student-made media can all help students understand their fellow beings in the world.

Students gain a sense of history when they visualize what a day would be like in the twelfth century; perhaps they might try living as if they were in the twelfth century for a day. Historical moments can be pantomimed to project nonverbally the feeling of the situation. Maps and globes are traditional visual materials used in world study. Encourage students to manipulate and construct maps and ask that they show as well as tell how to move from one point to another.

Summary

Integration of hemispheric skills and individual stimulation is the key to a balanced mode of thinking. Teachers can help promote balanced thought when they are aware of meeting the needs of both hemispheres and when they provide experiences that are designed to use both verbal and visual thinking. If a teacher is aware that a child has talents in a specialized mode and then asks the child to solve problems through a different mode, the child's frustration and difficulty can result in hostility toward the teacher or the learning process itself. This discouragement and hostility may be avoided if children are allowed to use their specialized talents.

An Evolution of Consciousness

The Suppressed Mode

It was stated previously that school curricula tend to suppress the holistic, simultaneous, and intuitive mode of consciousness whose functions are located mostly in the right hemisphere of the brain. The basic subjects in school have long been considered the linear subjects of reading, writing, and arithmetic to the neglect of nonlinear subjects such as art, dance, meditation, and media studies. The back-to-basics movement is a re-emphasis of the linear mode of thought. College entrance examinations, IQ tests, and, in general, the entire standardized testing program are linear. Not only does this testing program discriminate against a child who is not linearly oriented but it dictates linear and sequential instructional methods such as reading and writing. At the same time, it neglects and even suppresses holistic and intuitive right hemisphere functions.

The development of written English has also influenced the suppression of the simultaneous mode of consciousness. The English language uses primarily a linear/sequential pattern, which has stimulated the development of linear/sequential processes. People of other cultures whose language is visually oriented (right hemisphere dominant) do not show the same inclination toward linear/sequential processes. For example, spoken Japanese is represented by two symbol systems, Katakana and Kanji. Katakana and English are similar because sounds of the spoken language are represented in writing. In Kanji, however, the written symbol represents an idea, not a sound. If a Japanese-speaking person loses the use of the left hemisphere of the brain, he loses the ability to read and write in Katakana, but he does not lose the ability to read and write in Kanji. Apparently Kanji and other visual means of communication in which symbols represent ideas rather than sounds are situated in the right hemisphere of the brain, not the left as in English.

In addition to schools and language, other forces in the Western culture have stressed the linear mode. Instead of attempting to enumerate these many influences, it might be helpful to take an evolutionary look at man's relationship with nature. It is difficult to determine when the linear/rational mode began to exclude the holistic/simultaneous mode, but possibly it came about when people started to control and exploit nature and began to develop a technocratic and competitive society. Nature and natural processes are holistic, whereas the technocratic era is not. Before people started to exploit nature by abusing its resources, a harmony existed between man and nature. As people attempted to control natural patterns both within themselves and in the environment, linear/rational processes began to dominate and the holistic/simultaneous mode was ignored and subsequently suppressed. The processes of the technocratic era are "un-natural"; therefore, the linear/rational mode dominated and excluded the holistic mode of consciousness.

Consciousness Evolution

Despite efforts to suppress it, the holistic mode of consciousness is being revived and utilized. Now it appears that Western society is entering a new era in consciousness. Some indicators of this new era are a new or renewed interest in biofeedback, hypnosis, meditation, intuition, environmental issues, and man's relationship with nature. These will be explored in more detail in this section.

In the field of medicine, *biofeedback* is a recent development that utilizes the holistic mode in promoting healing. It consists of electronic monitoring of body temperatures, perspiration, and muscle tension, with the response fed back to the patient by audible cues. Biofeedback is used to relieve stress and anxiety that often cause pain. Once people become aware of the signs of tension, they may learn to relax.

Through the use of biofeedback apparatus, patients have been helped to reduce or prevent headaches, muscle pains, asthma, and other maladies. It has been reported that people have also learned to increase alpha brain waves, the brain rhythm associated with a feeling of relaxation and calmness.

Hypnosis has recently been explored as a means of helping people control bodily dysfunctions. In order for this control to take place, however, a person must be responsive to hypnosis, which is not always possible. Some medical hypnotists believe that the capacity to respond to hypnosis is directly related to simultaneous/holistic dominance and imagination, which seem to be lacking in the rational/linear dominant person, who tends to be more analytical. Under hypnotic suggestion the intuitive and holistic person can separate himself from the perception of pain.

Meditation of various kinds has been useful both in medicine and in expanding the consciousness. Meditation techniques generally involve a focus of attention. The focus varies, but it may be one's breathing, or concentrating on an item such as a doorknob, a single word, a candle flame, or a sound. The objective of the concentration is to narrow the point of focus to produce an altered awareness. Meditation has been helpful for some people in controlling hypertension, stuttering, anxiety, depression, allergies, and asthma. Also, practitioners of meditation claim aroused thoughts and sharpened insights through the production of alpha waves.

Intuition, an operation of the holistic right hemisphere, has often been characterized as "women's intuition." This phrase may have additional meaning when one considers that until very recent times women were generally denied access to higher education and many did not even attend secondary school. Perhaps the lack of formal schooling eliminated many of the opportunities to develop the linear and rational mode, so women developed the intuitive functions. Women's intuition, then, may have a basis of support in the split brain theory.

Although intuition may be dismissed as "unscientific," it is noted as a valid function by many creative people. Albert Einstein referred to the importance of intuitive thinking in his "Autobiographical Notes" when he wrote:

The connection of the latter (sense-experience) with the former (propositions) is purely intuitive, not itself of a logical nature. The degree of certainty with which this connection, viz., intuitive combination, can be undertaken, and nothing else, differentiates empty fantasy from scientific "truth." . . . This [indecision] was obviously due to the fact that my intuition was not strong enough in the field of mathematics in order to differentiate clearly the fundamentally important, that which is really basic, from the rest of the more or less dispensable erudition.

Finally, the *concern for environmental issues* is another indication of a shift to the holistic mode of consciousness. The rational/linear approach to problem solving has blinded people as they undertook technological advances without looking at the total scene. In the environment, linear answers have developed a path that could lead to society's extinction. Why was it not obvious to people that certain technological advances were leading to environmental extinction? Perhaps the emphasis on the linear, rational, and analytic process caused this problem. When the holistic mode re-emerged, it encouraged a new examination of the environmental issues. The linear/rational view was not adequate, but it was familiar and common at that time. Investigators have learned from their mistakes and now are employing the holistic mode in looking at the environmental situation.

When people were more involved and united with nature, the holistic mode coexisted with the linear/sequential mode. As technology advanced, the linear/sequential mode became dominant. If people are beginning to utilize the holistic mode again, a reunion with or a concern for nature should be evident. Currently there is a concern for the environment and a renewed interest in nature, as is evident from the increased activity of the National Geographic Society, the Audubon Society, and similar groups. Camping, backpacking, and other outdoor activities have grown in popularity. House plants are not new, but the current number of plant stores is without precedent. Outdoor gardens are also indicative of the return to nature and natural things and to a holistic view of life.

These emerging cultural changes indicate an increased awareness of the importance of the holistic mode of consciousness. The time is appropriate for this transformation. The linear/analytic mode is not being denied. Rather, the holistic mode is beginning to demonstrate some of the deficiencies brought about by linear/analytic dominance. One's view of the world should not be one-sided. It should be balanced and integrated.

Holistic Schooling

The back-to-basics movement assumes that concentration on reading, writing, and arithmetic will develop competent individuals. In line with the split brain theory, though, students will only be half-developed. An additional component is needed to develop the simultaneous and metaphoric processes. Formal schooling must stress both modes of consciousness.

Open education and confluent education are two examples of approaches in which the holistic mode is balanced with the linear mode. The open classroom is flexible, with space divided into learning centers rather than one fixed, homogeneous unit. Students are permitted to explore, individually or in groups, the classroom environment and decide what activities to undertake. Multimedia resources abound, with no reliance on one particular medium. The teacher's instruction is usually directed at small groups or individuals, seldom to the entire group. The open classroom allows students to develop their interests and to follow their intuition as the teacher assists in constructing an individualized curriculum for each student. In addition to learning the basics, students develop their right hemisphere functions through activities that emphasize holistic and simultaneous approaches.

George Brown, Mark Phillips, and Stewart Shapiro state in Phi Delta Kappa Fastback 85, *Getting It All Together: Confluent Education*, that confluent education blends

> . . . emotional and intellectual factors in learning and teaching or integrates the affective and cognitive domains. The affective domain deals with feelings, emotions, attitudes, values, and, perhaps, intuition and some aspects of creativity. The cognitive domain includes the intellectual functioning of the individual, not only what an individual learns but also the various intellectual processes of learning, from rote learning to learning how to learn.

Open and confluent education are two recent major instructional strategies that foster and integrate both modes of consciousness. However, their acceptance and utilization is far from being universal.

Other bimodal areas include instructional media that have integrated the two modes. Visual media stress the spatial and simultaneous processes of the right hemisphere as well as visual thinking. And because of the sequencing involved in most visual media (action in films, order of slides in slide-tape shows, etc.), the media tend to integrate the operations of the left and right hemispheres.

Educational research has begun to employ nonlinear methodology. William J. Tikunoff and others from the Far West Laboratory for Educational Research and Development have been examining ecologically based research that has a broader base than traditional linear research. They emphasize curriculum development that involves teachers, teacher educators, and researchers in a collaborative inquiry into teaching and learning that considers the classroom as an ecological unit. The May, 1977, edition of the *Anthropology and Education Quarterly* was devoted to the question of qualitative and quantitative research methodologies in education and the search for a common paradigm.

Some inroads have been made into the development and utilization of the holistic mode of consciousness. The next step is to assimilate the meaning of this evolution and to explore the possibilities for the integration of the two modes of consciousness.

Implications of the Consciousness Evolution

When right hemispheric functions are emphasized equally with left hemispheric functions, the next step is integration between the two hemispheres. There may be an overemphasis on expanding right hemispheric functions as this neglected hemisphere seeks parity with the left hemisphere. However, once this trend subsides, an integrated mode of consciousness will emerge. The combined mode will utilize both hemispheres individually as needed and will utilize the hemispheres jointly when appropriate. This practice will provide additional flexibility, increased awareness, and more total brain utilization.

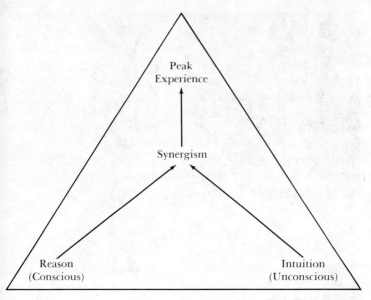

Modes of Awareness

The integrated mode of consciousness, by using both hemispheres jointly, will exhibit traits of unity, synthesis, and balance. Inappropriate, fragmented approaches to problems will be replaced by those that are holistic, but will include linear approaches that have prevailed until recently. The integrated mode of consciousness will not only provide new solutions, but will apply the balanced approach to problems that was previously lacking.

Employing the integrated modes of consciousness will result in the synergetic mode of consciousness that is reserved for peak experiences rather than for everyday experiences. The development of the synergetic mode of consciousness will induce additional peak experiences for more people and help them evolve into complete and whole human beings. The synergetic is at the top of this hierarchy of modes.

The unconscious level (in the diagram) is indicated by the right hemispheric function of intuition. The idea of this function is not

The sculpture "Synergism" by Severson and Schultz reflects synergetic balance and unity in a human experience.

new, but the intent is to give value to right hemispheric functions and to practice and utilize them. As the usage of the right hemispheric functions increases along with the already practiced functions of the left hemisphere (indicated by reason), increased occurrences of the synergetic mode of consciousness will occur. Reason and intuition synchronizing in those rare synergetic moments produce peak experiences. A person may write effective rhymes and rhythms but may lack the intuitive insights that make one poet great and another mediocre. It is the combination of the rational/linear skills and intuitive insights that produces great poetry through synergetic experiences.

The sight of a falling apple produced a peak experience for Isaac Newton. This happening possibly brought together for Newton his rational thoughts about motion and universal gravitation and intuitive insights about how this knowledge related to the planets. Newton reportedly had tremendous powers of concentration. His biographers report that linked with these powers of concentration was another gift—an intuitive sense for penetrating to the heart of a problem with no wasted effort. It seems that Newton was gifted with both reasoning and intuitive skills and utilized them fully in his extraordinary scientific discoveries.

The synergetic mode of consciousness operates infrequently but produces exciting results. The development of the previously neglected and undervalued right hemisphere is the catalyst that produces synergetic experiences. Increased traditional formal schooling is not necessarily important in this development. The implication for schools appears to be that nonlinear processes must also be stressed in the curriculum or students must search for them outside of the formal school setting.

Conclusion

Recent evidence from brain research has indicated that the brain consists of two hemispheres, right and left, that have distinct modes of consciousness. The left hemisphere specializes in linear, sequential, and analytical functions whereas the right hemisphere specializes in simultaneous, holistic, and visual/spatial functions. The linear mode has prevailed throughout the development of mankind, and since the rise of technocracy it has dominated. Recently, however, emphasis on the holistic mode has begun. Emergence of the holistic mode is slow because of the firm tradition of the linear mode. In addition, general thought is grounded in sequentiality through language, and people are usually comfortable with sequentiality. People are immersed in time, a linear function, and there is satisfaction in linearity because one knows what to expect. The split brain theory suggests that, in order to develop both hemispheres of the brain, attention must be given to holistic and intuitive functions both in and out of school.

People are beginning to recognize the limitations of analytic thought. The holistic mode is coming into prominence and is being used in problem-solving situations in order to gain a new perspective on the world. Educators need to recognize this need and the importance of the holistic mode and begin to emphasize the practice of non-linear functions in the school curriculum.

A rather speculative viewpoint suggests that, when the two hemispheres begin operating in balance and are used appropriately, a synergetic mode of consciousness will appear more frequently. This synrgetic mode will form peak experiences when the holistic and linear modes are synchronized. The result is a rare moment when "everything clicks" and new knowledge is created.

Many further questions need to be probed. How do the two hemispheres relate to each other in such subjects as math, reading, art, music? Does the interaction of the two hemispheres inhibit learning at times? What implications, if any, does the new brain research have for the memory process? Do the functions that are the specialty of the left hemisphere require more conscious cultivation than right hemispheric activities? Is discovery encouraged by stressing linearity?

The exploration of this area of knowledge has just begun. Although results of recent brain research are encouraging and relate directly to education, much more work is needed to evaluate the speculative areas noted here. Furthermore, it should be recognized that this research offers no panacea for education's ills; it does provide an avenue for increased instructional effectiveness and student achievement.

Selected References

Arnheim, Rudolf. *Visual Thinking*. Los Angeles: University of California Press, 1969.
   Arnheim's thesis is that all thinking is basically perceptual, both in art and science. Visual thinking is the means by which we derive ideas and, therefore, language.
Bogen, Joseph E. "Some Educational Aspects of Hemispheric Specialization." *UCLA Educator*, Spring, 1975, pp. 132-43.
   Bogen examines some of the implications for education that split brain research has produced.
Ferguson, Marilyn. *The Brain Revolution*. New York: Taplinger Publishing Company, Inc., 1973.
   An easy-to-read book that discusses the frontiers of mind research, including consciousness and brain damage.
Gazzaniga, Michael S. "Review of the Split Brain." *UCLA Educator*, Spring, 1975, pp. 9-12.

This issue of the *UCLA Educator* has several outstanding articles on education and the brain. In this article, Gazzaniga reviews the discovery of the split brain theory.

McKim, Robert H. *Experiences in Visual Thinking*. Monterey, California: Brooks/Cole, 1972.

McKim has taken many of the ideas associated with the right hemisphere and has built a course on visual thinking around them. This book illustrates many activities that employ visual thinking.

Ornstein, Robert E. *The Mind Field*. New York: Viking Press, 1976.

Ornstein, Robert E. *The Psychology of Consciousness*. New York: Penguin Books, 1972.

Ornstein is a leader in the study of consciousness. *Psychology of Consciousness* is a comprehensive work on the subject. *Mind Field*, a more recent book, is an outstanding treatment of meditation, psychiatry, Sufism, intuition, and many other subjects.

Samples, Bob. *The Metaphoric Mind*. Reading, Massachusetts: Addison-Wesley Publishing Company, 1976.

Samples's well-illustrated book celebrates the metaphoric mind, the ignored right half of the brain. Samples argues for a balance between the two halves of the brain.

Sperry, Roger W. "Left-Brain, Right-Brain." *Saturday Review*, August 9, 1975, pp. 30-33.

This issue of *Saturday Review* presents several articles on the brain. Sperry, an early researcher of the split brain theory, discusses some of his research.